The res
Endcliffe Park in Sheffield

For Leo Madoc Taylor
Born 12th August 2018

The Little Urban Fox Series

Book 1
The Little Urban Fox Explores Endcliffe Park Sheffield

www.littleurbanfoxandfriends.co.uk

Story copyright 2019 © Helen Stokes
Illustration copyright 2019 © Kathryn Herold

The rights of Helen Stokes & Kathryn Herold and their work has been asserted by them in accordance with the
Copyright, Design Patent Act 1988

January 2019

ISBN: 978-1-906722-60-9

Published by Arc Publishing and Print
166 Knowle Lane
Sheffield
S11 9SJ

t: 07809 172872   e: chris@arcbooks.co.uk   w: sheffieldbooks.co.uk

The Little Urban Fox awoke from his sleep in the den under an old oak tree in Endcliffe Park. His mother hadn't returned from her night-time hunting, and the Little Fox thought that he might go out to look for her. He was eager to see more of the world and wanted an adventure.

His brothers were fast asleep in their cosy bed as the Little Fox peeked out of the entrance to his home, between the twisted tree roots.

3

The Little Fox had not been out alone in the park before, so off he went in search of his mother.

As he moved away from the path and into the trees, he saw a hedgehog snuffling about amongst the crunchy autumn leaves near a tall stone reaching up to the sky.

ERECTED
TO COMMEMORATE
THE JUBILEE
OF
QUEEN VICTORIA
1887

"Excuse me," the Little Fox said politely.
"Have you seen Mother Fox pass by?"

The hedgehog looked up in surprise, for it wasn't often
a fox stopped to speak to him.
"I've not seen anyone today," answered the
hedgehog. "I should ask the Great Queen,
she is very important and knows everything
that happens in this park. This tall
stone was put here especially
for her," he added. "Just
follow the path and you will
find her."

ERECTED
TO COMMEMORATE
THE JUBILEE
OF
QUEEN VICTORIA
1887

The Little Fox thanked his prickly new pal and silently slunk across the park to the footpath and the Great Queen ahead.

As he followed the path past the playground, he came to a grassy area where the Great Queen stood.

When the Little Fox looked up and saw the queen towering above him, he was too scared to speak, for though she looked down on him with kindly eyes, she was so tall. It seemed to the Little Fox that she nearly reached the sky.

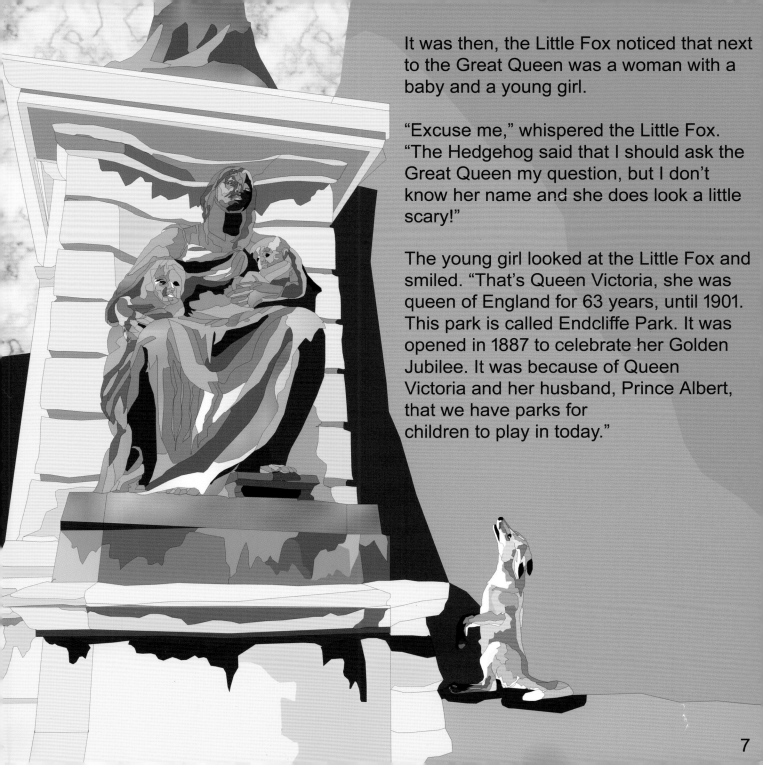

It was then, the Little Fox noticed that next to the Great Queen was a woman with a baby and a young girl.

"Excuse me," whispered the Little Fox. "The Hedgehog said that I should ask the Great Queen my question, but I don't know her name and she does look a little scary!"

The young girl looked at the Little Fox and smiled. "That's Queen Victoria, she was queen of England for 63 years, until 1901. This park is called Endcliffe Park. It was opened in 1887 to celebrate her Golden Jubilee. It was because of Queen Victoria and her husband, Prince Albert, that we have parks for children to play in today."

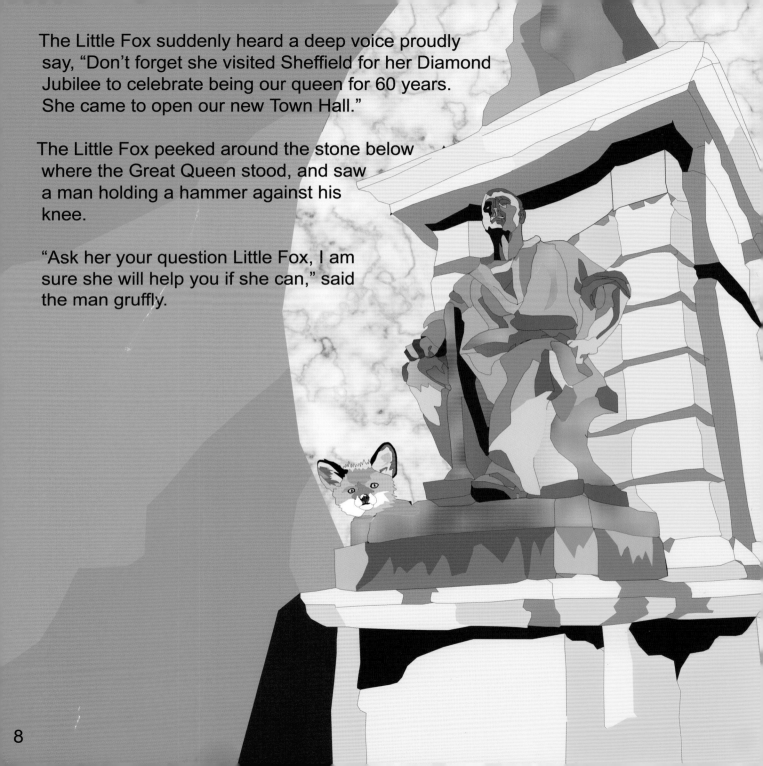

The Little Fox suddenly heard a deep voice proudly say, "Don't forget she visited Sheffield for her Diamond Jubilee to celebrate being our queen for 60 years. She came to open our new Town Hall."

The Little Fox peeked around the stone below where the Great Queen stood, and saw a man holding a hammer against his knee.

"Ask her your question Little Fox, I am sure she will help you if she can," said the man gruffly.

The Little Fox took a deep breath and pointed his muzzle up to the sky where the Great Queen stood above him.

"Excuse me, Great Queen Victoria. Have you seen Mother Fox pass this way?"

"I have seen a lot of things," answered the queen in a regal voice.

"I did see a very handsome red fox slink past earlier. She was going towards the café looking for supper to give her cubs."

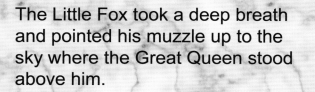

ERECTED
BY
CITIZENS SHEFFIELD
IN MEMORY OF
A
GREAT QUEEN

MDCCCIV

9

The Little Fox gave a deep bow and thanked the Great Queen for helping him. He thought his mother couldn't be far away, as it was not long since the Great Queen had seen her.

He ran back up the path towards the café, with his bushy red tail bobbing up and down behind him.

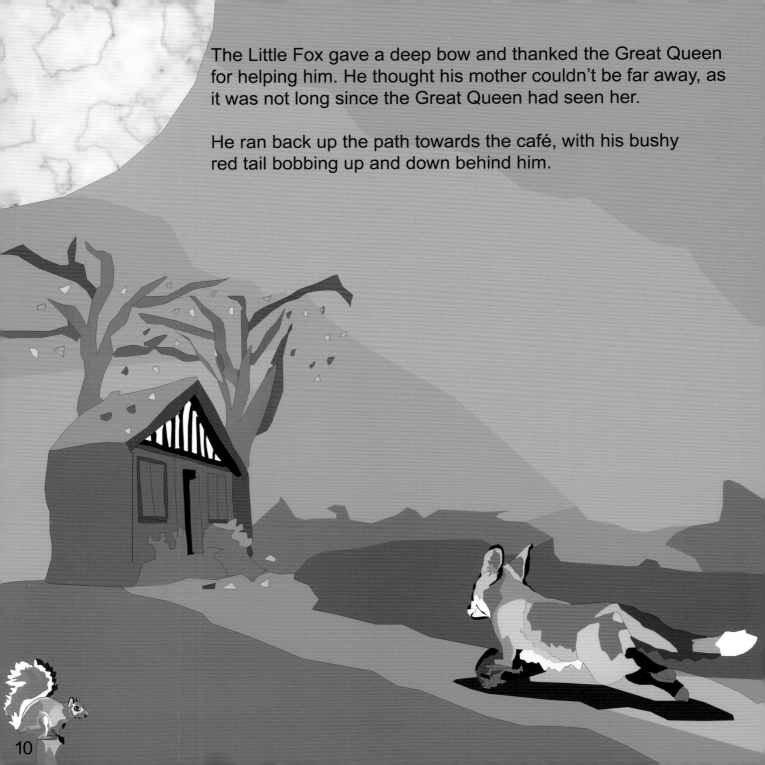

Before long, the Little Fox met a huge brown toad who
seemed to be reading from a large book that lay before him.
"Excuse me, Mr. Toad," said the Little Fox politely. "Have you
seen Mother Fox pass this way?"

The toad looked down at the Little Fox, feeling put out to have been disturbed.
He grunted, in a rather 'pig-like' manner,
"I did see a fine-looking fox crossing the stepping stones over
the River Porter to Mi Amigo some hours ago.
That may have been Mother Fox going to pay her respects."

The Little Fox wasn't sure what the old toad meant, but he could see the stepping stones ahead of him, so he thanked the toad and hurried on his way.

The Little Fox skipped lightly across the 11 stones over the river, and climbed the bank to where the American Oak trees stood proudly before him, majestic with their leaves of gold and brown.

The Little Fox looked
around him and saw
a large stone, at the foot of
which lay wreaths of flowers. He
moved closer to get a better look, hoping
his mother may be there, as the Little Fox had
heard that all mothers like flowers.

As he rushed towards the flowers he almost
trod on a little grey rabbit, half hidden
amongst the leaves.

"Excuse me," said the Little Fox, "The Great Queen and the toad told me that they had seen Mother Fox come this way and I wondered if she had been to look at the flowers?"

The rabbit eyed the Little Fox warily, wondering if he was about to become his breakfast. Deciding that the Little Fox looked a trustworthy fellow, the rabbit, his whiskers quivering, answered, "I try to avoid foxes, I know that they are very fond of rabbits, but I am looking forward to growing up one day."

" Oh dear," said the Little Fox, "I was hoping you could help me. Do you know why all these flowers are here?"

The grey rabbit answered wisely, "They are here for the brave American Airforce men. Every year lots of people come and lay flowers to remember the day, 22nd February 1944, when the pilot, John Kreigshauser, crashed his plane of 10 men returning from a battle in World War 2."

"But why did he crash into the trees when there is a big field down there where he could have landed?" asked the Little Fox, pointing to the park behind him.

The grey rabbit answered, with a tear in his eye, "His plane was in trouble, and he may have run out of fuel as he needed to land. It is said that he could have landed safely on the grass, but he wanted to avoid the children playing in the park, so he crashed into the trees on the hillside. His family were given a medal after he died, for what he did."

"He must have been very brave," said the little Fox, his voice a little gruff from emotion. "I hope that I am as brave as that one day."

The grey rabbit looked thoughtfully at the Little Fox, thinking that one day he may indeed become very brave. Then he suggested that the Little Fox might go up the river in search of his mother.

The grey rabbit knew that there were lots of ducks swimming in the water and he had heard that foxes were very fond of ducks….

By now it was getting light, and sunlight shone down between the trees.

Cyclists were pedalling on the paths, joggers ran by, and dogs were scampering along the river bank.

17

Excited to explore the new smells of the fresh autumn morning, the Little Fox lifted his nose and sniffed the aromas of breakfast cooking in the nearby café. He retraced his footsteps back across the stepping stones and squeezed through the railings behind the café.

By now, the smell of bacon cooking, and the sound of it sizzling in the pan, were almost overwhelming for the Little Fox and he licked his lips greedily. He crept up to a nearby bin and nudged the lid off with his nose. Inside he saw a wonderful sight of leftover food, and he jumped into the bin and filled his stomach without delay.

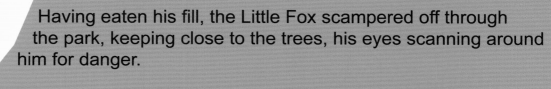

Having eaten his fill, the Little Fox scampered off through the park, keeping close to the trees, his eyes scanning around him for danger.

When he came to a millpond he looked around for his mother, but she was nowhere to be seen.

The ducks on the edge of the pond quickly leapt into the water as he approached and, as hard as he tried, none would come near enough for him to speak to them.

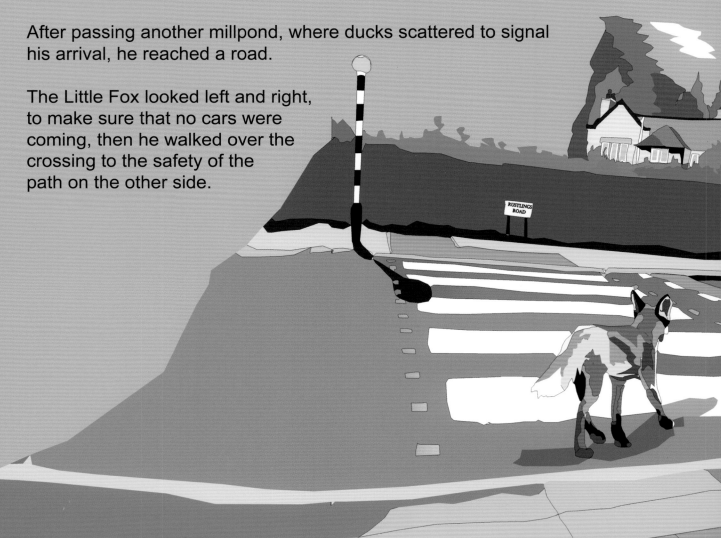

With a full belly, the Little Fox was quite enjoying his adventure and he was keen to find out more about this place where he lived.

After passing another millpond, where ducks scattered to signal his arrival, he reached a road.

The Little Fox looked left and right, to make sure that no cars were coming, then he walked over the crossing to the safety of the path on the other side.

RUSTLINGS ROAD

A little further along the path, he came to an old building.

The Little Fox climbed curved millstone steps to a little red door, just above which was the roof of the building. The Little Fox jumped, up over the door, and onto the roof beyond.

As he looked down, he could see a huge wooden wheel, dripping with water but standing still in the crisp November morning.

The Little Fox thought the building may be a good place to rest, if only he could find a way in.

Remembering that the little red door had been left ajar, he gently pushed it with his nose and quietly crept inside.

Looking around, the Little Fox saw stone wheels, straps,
and wooden blocks worn with age.

He saw an old sack in one dark corner of the building and, tired as
he was, he wearily curled up beneath it.

Just as he was drifting off to sleep, his nose was tickled.
He opened one eye to see a huge spider staring down on him.

"Hello, Madam Spider," said the Little Fox, aware
that spiders must be treated with great respect.
"I was wondering what this building is;
It seems a very old place, do you
mind if I sleep here?"

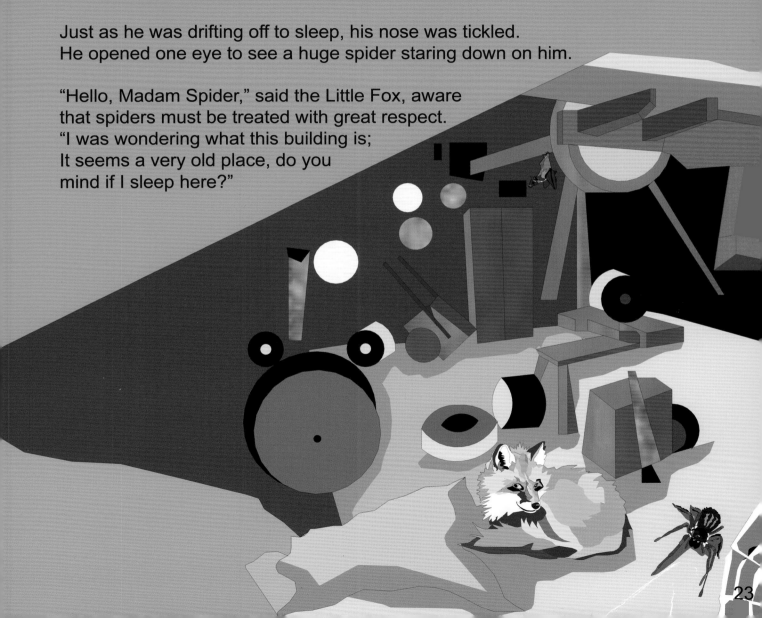

The spider, despite having eight legs and being a little bit hairy, was very friendly. She spoke softly to the Little Fox, "My family have always lived here. It's called Shepherd Wheel after a man called Mr. Shepherd who employed 10 men here in the year 1784."

Seeing that the Little Fox seemed very interested, the spider went on, "I have heard tales of cutlers who forged their own blades before bringing them here to sharpen them on the grinding wheels."

"That sounds like dangerous work," said the Little Fox.

"I don't think it was a very safe place to be in those days. I have heard that children as young as 10 were employed here," the spider replied solemnly.

"Shepherd Wheel is a museum now though," said the spider more cheerfully. "It is a very interesting place to live".

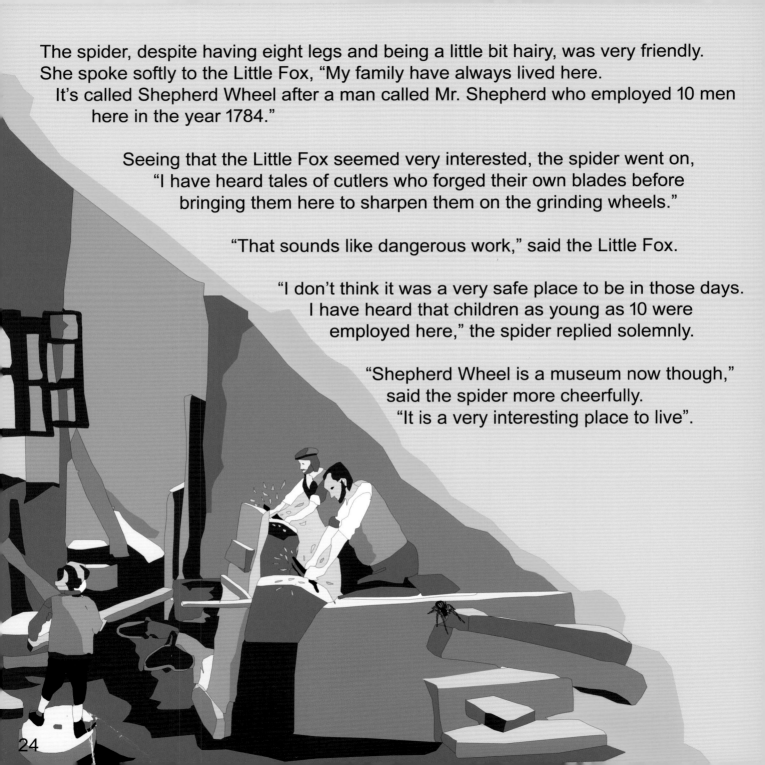

The Little Fox looked worried; he didn't want anyone to find him here or to start 'grinding' blades when he was around!

"Don't worry," said the spider. "You will be safe here today, I will keep watch. Go to sleep Little Fox."

With that, the Little Fox snuggled down to sleep, dreaming of the further adventures he would have when he awoke in the evening.

As the Little Fox lay dreaming, his mother, having found her cub, jumped in through the window and kissed the Little Fox on his head.

He stirred in his sleep and heard his mother's voice. "Sleep well little one, It is time for you to go out into the world and make your own adventures. I will see you again very soon."

And with that, Mother Fox jumped back through the window and disappeared into the nearby woods. The Little Fox smiled contentedly and fell back into a deep sleep.

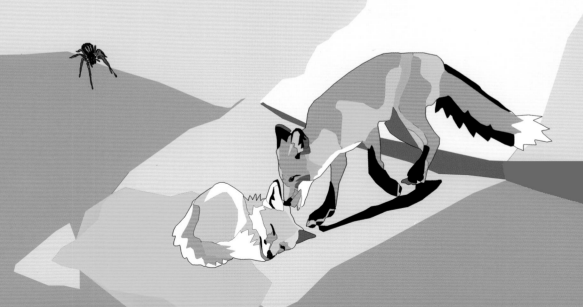

Endcliffe Park and Queen Victoria

Endcliffe Park was opened in 1887 to commemorate the Jubilee of Queen Victoria. The land was purchased by Sheffield Corporation from the trustees of Mr Robert Younge for £5323. This was to provide a public park and to lay a sewer to prevent health risks.

In the park there are two monuments dedicated to Queen Victoria.

Queen Victoria believed in people working hard and looking after their families.

Stone marking the opening of the park.

Obelisk commemorating the Jubilee of Queen Victoria.

Maternity: A mother holding a baby, with her other arm around a child.

Statue of Queen Victoria with 'Maternity' and 'Labour' at either side.

Labour: A working man sat on an anvil holding a sledgehammer.

Toad Sculpture

Near the café and children's playground is a carved wooden toad sculpture, reading a book on which is the limerick:

> There once was a man in the park,
> Who stepped on a toad in the dark,
> He heard it go squelch,
> Let out a loud belch,
> And said "what a curious lark".

Porter Brook and Millponds

Porter Brook is a river that runs through Endcliffe Park, coming from its source on Burbidge Moors before flowing on down to the River Sheaf at the train station.

Within Endcliffe Woods, there are several millponds which were part of the industrial past of the valley where the river was dammed to provide power to grinding mills. Further up the valley you can find Shepherd Wheel, Wiremill Dam and Forge Dam. When the park was built, William Goldring adapted the dams for bathing, skating, and waterbirds.

Stepping Stones near Endcliffe Park Café

The stepping stones across Porter Brook are worn with age from the many people who have used them for over 120 years. They were put in place when the park was created. At the same time the river was stocked with trout.

Shepherd Wheel

- Shepherd Wheel dates back to the 1500's as a workshop where cutlers and grinders worked to produce sharp blades. In the 1930's the wheel's role in the Sheffield cutlery industry ended.

- The waterwheel was powered by water from the dam above.

- It is said that the wheel was left by William Beighton to his sons in 1584.

- Mr Shepherd held the tenancy in 1794 and the wheel is named after him.

- From 1820 to 1930, the wheel was owned by the Hinde family until its closure in 1930.

- Up to 10 men could work at the grinding wheels, and records indicate that children as young as 10 worked there.

- The working conditions could have caused silicosis or asthma from all the grinding dust.

- In 1900, Whitely Woods were bought by Sheffield City Council to make a public park.

- The wheel was restored and opened as a museum in 1962, and closed in 1997.

- Since 1998, Sheffield Museum's Trust has owned Shepherd Wheel.

- The Museum was re-opened in 2012, with funding from the Heritage Lottery Fund, Shefffield City Council, and Friends of Porter Valley.

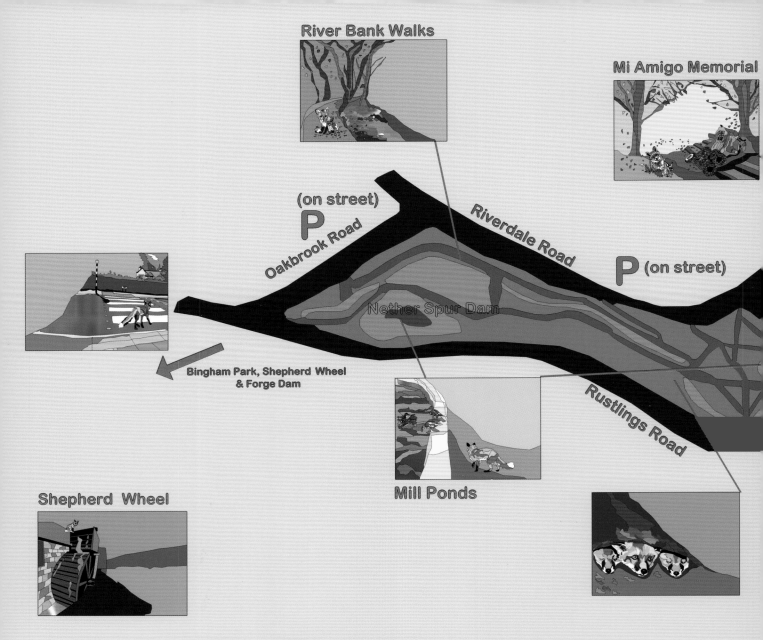

River Bank Walks

Mi Amigo Memorial

(on street)

P

Oakbrook Road

Riverdale Road

P (on street)

Nether Spur Dam

Rustlings Road

Bingham Park, Shepherd Wheel
& Forge Dam

Mill Ponds

Shepherd Wheel

Endcliffe Park Map
Sheffield

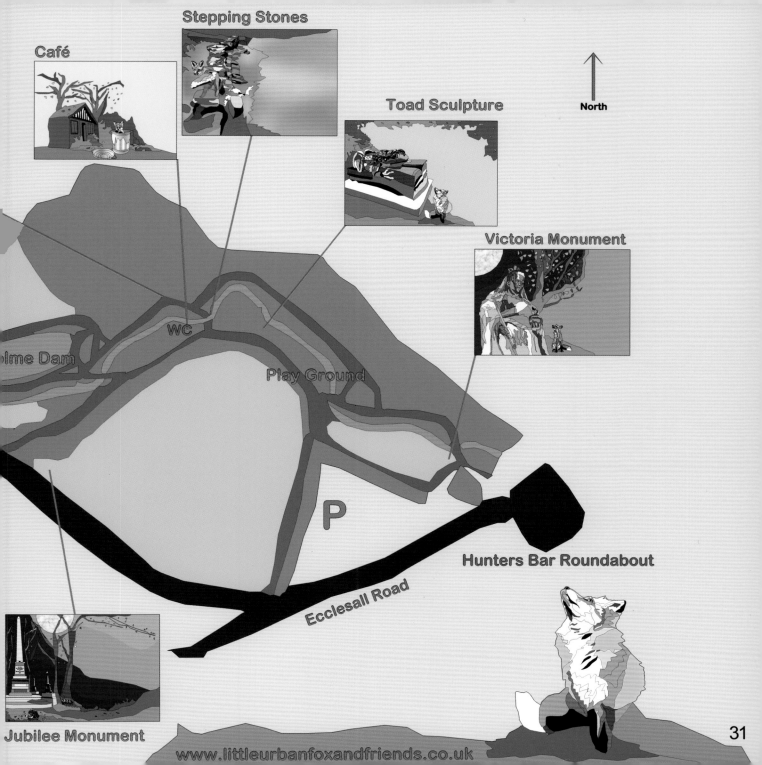

Café

Stepping Stones

Toad Sculpture

North

Victoria Monument

WC

olme Dam

Play Ground

P

Hunters Bar Roundabout

Ecclesall Road

Jubilee Monument

31

www.littleurbanfoxandfriends.co.uk

The Mi Amigo War Memorial

Mi Amigo was an American B17 bomber plane in World War II, piloted by Lt. John Kriegshauser, who was 23 years old.

Returning from a mission over Denmark, with the plane badly damaged, the pilot needed to land. Seeing playing fields in Endcliffe park, the plane started to come down. The pilot avoided the nearby houses, and children playing in the park, to crash land in the trees at 5pm on Tuesday 22nd February 1944.

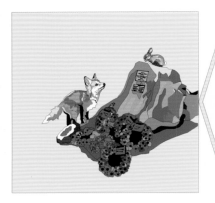

All of the 10 crew were killed in the crash. Twenty firefighters worked to put out the fire, using water pumped from the Porter Brook.

The pilot was posthumously awarded the Distinguished Flying Cross for his bravery in ensuring that no-one in the park or homes around were killed.

Ten American Oak trees were planted at the site of the crash and in 1969 a commemorative stone was placed there. An annual remembrance ceremony is held at the site on the Sunday closest to 22nd February to this day.

The full story of 'Mi-Amigo' is told in a book published in June 2014 on Amazon Kindle by local military historian Paul Allonby, called 'Courage Above the Clouds'.